Contents

Say the sounds

s a t p i n d g o c
ck e u r h b f ff l

On the bus

Dad and I got the bus.

Off the bus

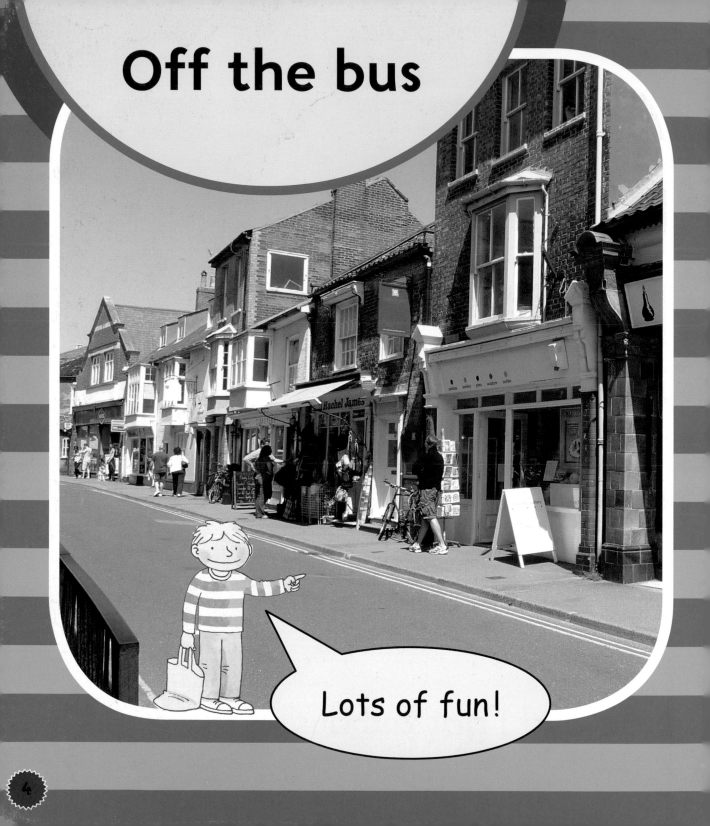

top

socks

I had to get a top
and lots of socks.

top ✓
socks ✓
bag
pens
pad

top ✓
socks ✓
bag ✓
pens
pad

bag

I got a red bag.

I got a big pad and
lots of pens in a pot.

Back on the bus

Dad and I had to run to get the bus back!

Glossary

 bag

 bus

 pad

 pen

 pot

 sock